TOWN SMALL

written and illustrated by
Lolly Stoddard

Town Small is a special town
where the streets get full
and people come from
everywhere
to visit.

The summer months make
Town Small seem so big;
there are street parades,
boat parades,
an art show...

and a bridge that goes up every hour to let the boats pass by.

When the bridge goes up,
Town Small seems to grow even bigger.
All the cars have to stop,
people walking have to wait,
the bicycles stand still,
and everyone enjoys watching
the boats go by.

There is a special place within Town Small
unlike any other place at all.
It is a small town inside Town Small
where fun days are like the old
times of long ago.

There are old whaling boats,
old sailing boats...

old rowing boats, a tug,
and boats that take you
through the bridge!

This small town inside Town Small
becomes my own special playground,
with picnic days and old-fashioned games
and a secret place for children only.

I can dress up to pretend with my friends,
while my sisters learn to sail
and my brothers gaze among the stars.

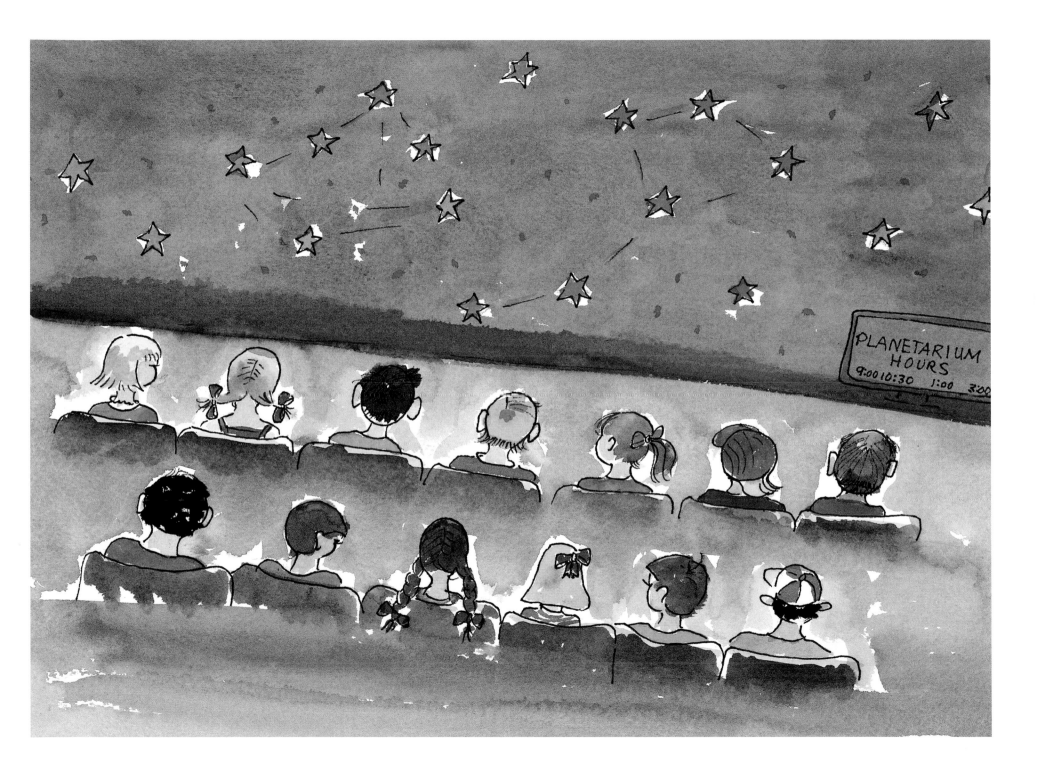

Each year, after the calendar
reads September,
the visiting people begin to head home
and Town Small enjoys becoming
small again.

The bridge seems to slow down
for just a little while.

Yet, before we know it,
the Hallowe'en Parade is here.

Time passes quickly and
Santa Claus arrives by tugboat.

We sing holiday carols...

and soon the bridge begins to make
Town Small seem big again!

Experiencing her home town through the eyes of her three
now-grown children was the springboard for the story Town Small.
Lolly lives near Mystic, Connecticut, with her husband, Duncan,
and paints local scenes of the New England shore.

Book design by Linda Cusano
Printed in China